A WORLD FULL OF HOMES

A WORLD
FULL OF HOMES

By WILLIAM A. BURNS

Assistant to Director, American Museum of Natural History

Pictures by PAULA HUTCHISON

Illustration Corps, American Museum of Natural History

McGRAW-HILL BOOK COMPANY

NEW YORK TORONTO LONDON

A WORLD FULL OF HOMES

17181920 HDBP 75432

For Rita and for Michael

Snow Igloo

Contents

Yurt

Unusual homes

How would you like to live in a home made of blocks of snow? The Eskimos do, and like it. Or would you like to live in a house made of paper? The Japanese have for hundreds of years, and find them very comfortable. Perhaps you have already lived in a trailer, but gypsies lived and traveled in wagons long years before America was discovered.

There are many unusual homes around the world. We call them unusual only because they seem strange to us when we compare them with our own houses. They are not unusual to people who live in them. These strange homes serve those who live in them exactly as our familiar homes do — they protect the people from heat and cold, rain and snow, sun and wind. They give the people who live in them a place where they can eat, cook, bathe, sleep, work, study, and visit with their families and their friends. They are the same as our houses, even though they may look different.

We know that people always took simple materials that were close to them to build their homes. If grass was near, they built with grass. If caves were

9

close by, they lived in the caves. When they lived near forests, they used trees, branches, twigs, leaves, bark, or wood to build their homes. When they lived near clay deposits, they made brick houses. Those who could find stone, used stone.

But sometimes they had to use materials that seem strange to us. Sometimes they had to use familiar materials in a strange way. People who build unusual houses have good reasons for making them that way. Some have to travel long distances to find food for themselves or for their animals. They cannot make permanent homes. Others have no wood or clay but can find plenty of small stones to build with. Still others live where their work takes them — in lighthouses or in boats or barges.

We'll begin this story of how people have lived by first visiting unusual homes. Later we'll go so far back in time that we'll find that man did not even know how to build at all. Step by step, we'll follow people and see how they learned to make themselves a place in which to live, finding new materials, new tools, new inventions, new ideas about how to live. Now let's look at nomads.

Nomads are people who do not stay in one place all of the time. They must move on to find grass enough for their animals. If they do not raise animals, they must move when the animals they hunt for food go to another place. Their houses must be simple enough to put up and take down quickly. They must be light in weight so that the people can carry them easily from place to place. They must be warm enough to keep the nomads comfortable in winter. They must be cool in hot weather. The nomads need light, movable homes.

The Indians who lived on the American plains, long before Columbus came, were nomads. They followed the great herds of buffalo that roamed the plains. When the buffaloes moved on in search of new grass, the Indians had to pack up and move on too. They needed the buffalo for food, clothing, and for material to make their tents they called tipis [tee-pees].

Except along some of the rivers, there was little wood growing on the plains. The summers were hot and the winters were bitter cold. So the Indians made tall cone-shaped tents of the skin of the buffalo. When they wanted to build a tipi, they set long poles in a circle. The poles were lashed at the top to keep them together. Then they stretched tanned buffalo skins, with the hair scraped off, over the poles. They pegged down the bottoms of the skins to keep the wind and the dust out. A flap at the top of the tipi let their cooking smoke out. Sometimes they put up a low inner wall of skins to keep the wind from blowing on them.

It did not take long to set up a tipi or to take it down. When the buffalo herds moved, the Indians struck their tipis and followed. When the herds stopped, the Indians quickly put up their skin tipis. Before Indians got horses from the Spaniards, they used dogs to help them move their belongings. They tied trailing sticks to the dogs' backs and put some of their goods across the sticks. When they got horses from the Spaniards, they tied long poles to the horses' backs and were then able to drag heavy loads. They did not know how to make a wheel, but they did know that more weight could be dragged by man or animal than could be carried on their backs.

You can make a model of a Plains Indian tipi by getting about a dozen smooth sticks a foot long and stripping the bark off. Then cross two of them about an inch from the top and tie them. Put the rest of the sticks in the fork you have made by tying the first two sticks, then tie the other sticks to make a cone-shaped circular frame. Instead of buffalo skins, you can use an old piece of sheet to cover the frame. Leave an opening flap for a door and also an opening at the top where the smoke can escape. Later, you might

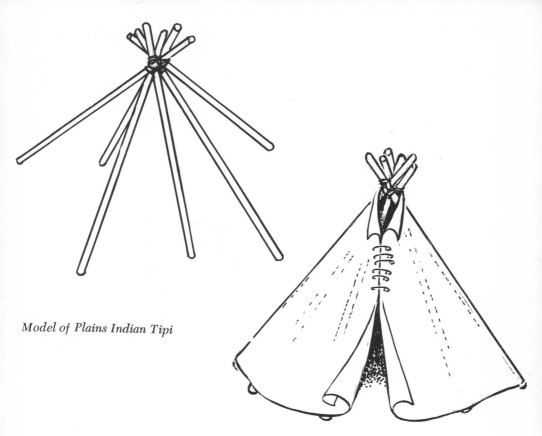

Model of Plains Indian Tipi

want to try a full-sized tipi to play in. If you do, you make it the same way as you made the model. But you had better use stronger cloth than torn pieces of bed sheet. An old canvas awning or a large piece of bed ticking will make a fine tipi. (See diagrams above.)

Another nomadic people live behind the Himalayan Mountains in Tibet. These people keep sheep and yaks. The yak is a big animal with long woolly hair. When the Tibetan nomads stay in one place too long their animals eat all the grass and moss. So they, like the Plains Indians, have to find new grass and moss for their stock.

Like the Indians, their home is easily put up and taken down. It is called a yurt. A yurt is a lattice-framed dwelling, covered with heavy felt mats. The felt is made from the wool taken from the yak. To make felt, the people spread the wool on the ground. They roll it and flatten it until it mats together. When it is all one strong piece it is called felt.

Winter in Tibet is very cold and bitter. The winds are strong and piercing. But the thick felt yurt keeps the people as warm as toast. It is smoky, however, because the yurt has no hole to let the smoke out. Even a small hole lets too much cold air in.

Many desert people are nomads. They raise sheep, goats, and camels. Like other wandering people, they need fresh pasturage for their flocks. They cannot carry heavy belongings or shelters. Because they live in a warm climate their tents are made of cloth. Sometimes they weave the material for their tents from goat hair.

From the hot desert to the icy cold of Eskimo country is quite a jump. But some Eskimos are like nomads because they must go long distances to hunt for food. They have permanent summer homes made

Eskimo Sod Home

of wood, stone, or earth. But on hunting trips they make a most unusual home — the snow igloo.

In the Eskimo language, the word "igloo" means house, not snow house. All Eskimo houses or shelters are igloos. When the Eskimo makes a snow igloo he must have snow of the right kind. He tests it by sticking the handle of his spear into it. If it is just right for building, he cuts out blocks with a knife made of walrus ivory. Snow does not stick to such a knife.

He fits the first row of snow blocks into a circle. Then, standing inside, he builds the walls of the snow house. Each row of blocks slants toward him until he is sealed into a dome of snow blocks. With his ivory knife he cuts a door and crawls out. Sometimes he makes a window. There is no glass to be had, so the Eskimo chops out a windowpane of clear ice with his spear. He fits this window into his house and puts the piece he cut out on the side of the window to catch light to be reflected inside.

The Eskimo family sleeps inside the snow igloo on a platform of snow. They all huddle together on warm furs and they pull fur blankets over themselves. It is warm inside the house, so warm in fact that the family must take off its fur clothing. Cooking is done on a stone stove that burns seal fat, or blubber. The oil seeps up through wicks made of moss. It may be a little smoky inside, but that does not matter much when the temperature outside may go as low as eighty degrees below zero!

Because they live in a cold climate, the Eskimos eat much meat and fat. They catch seals and walruses with harpoons. They catch fish with hooks and nets. They can catch birds by cutting a hole in the roof of the snow house. Food is placed on the rim of the hole. When the birds light to eat the food, the Eskimo hunter grabs them by the legs and pulls them inside. Birds are also caught in nets on long poles.

Here, in their snug winter home, the Eskimo family keeps its food, spears, furs, and supplies. The members of the family carve toys and tools from bone and ivory. They tan skins for warm waterproof clothing and boots.

The Eskimo, hunting away from his permanent home in winter, has absolutely nothing to build with but snow. There are no trees, no grass, no stones, no mud, no sod. But there is plenty of snow, and the Eskimo has used it cleverly to keep his family safe and warm until they go back to their other house when hunting is good.

There are two ways for boys and girls to make a snow igloo. One is the way the Eskimo makes his home, but using a straight-edged shovel instead of a knife. But it is easier to get your friends to-gether after a good snowfall and make a big mound of snow, about six feet high. You must pack the

Snow Igloo Model

snow down to make it hard. Then, with a small shovel, you dig out the inside carefully, making sure that you do not make the walls too thin. When you have dug out your igloo you can sit in it. You can even cut a small window in it to let in more light. If the weather is very cold, you can throw water over it to put a coating of ice on it. You will be surprised how warm it feels inside the igloo, even in very cold weather.

Again and again, we see how people use what they find for building. In the southern part of Italy there is a great deal of loose stone. The Italians who live here make interesting "beehive" houses of it. They have so much loose stone around that they do not know what to do with all of it. They pick up the stones out of their fields so they can grow their crops. They make stone walls around every field. They even pile the stones in the center of the fields to get rid of them. And they make their houses, roofs and all, from these flat stones.

The man who makes a stone "beehive" house works a little like an Eskimo building with snow blocks. He builds his stone walls around in a circle until they come almost to a point at the top. These walls are often seven feet thick. The Italian home-maker does not use mortar or cement to hold the

Italian "Beehive" Home

stones together. They are laid "dry." But there is no danger that they will fall in on the family inside. The beehive builder does not cut his windows out after the house is made. He leaves narrow openings in the stone walls to serve as windows. He also makes a low, narrow door for his family to use.

If the owner of a "beehive" house does not sweep off his roof once in a while, dust will gather on it. After a time he will find grass and flowers growing on his roof. Some of these stone houses look like giant plants from a distance because of the grass and flowers on top.

The inside of the stone house is dark. The few

windows built into it are narrow and the sun must travel as far as seven feet to get inside. To make it lighter, the people often plaster the inside walls a gleaming white. This white plaster reflects the little light that manages to come through.

Even the beds are built into the thick walls. The floor is made of large flat pieces of stone. To make them easier on the feet, the mother scatters rushes or grass on the stone.

Finally, the stables for the animals and even the chicken coops are made of stones that otherwise would be a nuisance to the people who live in this part of Italy.

We usually think of a home as being on dry land or at least over land. But many thousands of Chinese

people are born on river boats and never leave them during their lifetime. The reason for living on the rivers and harbors is not clear. Some people say that Chinese land taxes were too high. To avoid paying them, the people lived on the rivers and in the harbors.

A Chinese river boat is about twenty feet long. It has a cabin for passengers, but the family lives in the stern, or the back, of the boat. Here they eat, sleep, and prepare their meals.

At Canton, China, more than two hundred and fifty thousand Chinese live on boats. They have their own floating stores that sell food, clothing, household articles, medicine, and even jewelry. Sometimes there are so many boats next to one an-

Chinese River Boats

other that you could almost walk across a river or a harbor by stepping from one to the other.

Young children who live on the river are kept from falling overboard by means of a rope that their mother ties around their waists. Older children sometimes wear a hollow gourd that will keep them floating if they should lose their balance and fall into the water.

Many other countries have people who live on the water. Here in America we have houseboats, complete with practically all the comforts of a house on land. Whole families live on river barges that carry lumber and bricks to big cities. The children on these houseboats and barges go to school in the

House Boat

Lighthouse

winter and spend their summers traveling on the water. When a barge ties up alongside one of our waterfront docks, you can see the bright living quarters. Curtains hang at the windows and boxes of geraniums bloom on their sills. Lines of wash flap in the river wind and the children play on deck as if in a back yard.

Not too many people live in lighthouses, but the few who do call them home. Some lighthouses are built on land and are not very different from ordinary houses. But some are perched on islands or on dangerous rocky shoals. When storms come up, a house at the foot of the light would be swept away by the giant waves. Then the keeper and his family, if he has one, live in the lighthouse itself.

There are no corners in a lighthouse because the building is round. Old-fashioned lighthouses depended on oil for the light and for the family lamps. Newer lights are run by gasoline-powered machines that make electricity. All food except fish must come from the shore. Once a week or so, either the family goes ashore to shop or a boat comes out with food for them. People who need to go to the movies much would find living in a lighthouse rather dull. But radio and television, together with work and books, make even lighthouse living enjoyable.

How would you like to live in a house made of paper? Many Japanese families like it. Japan is

Inside A Paper House

often shaken by earthquakes. Heavy houses made of wood or of brick might fall on them and injure them. But a light paper-and-wood house stands an earthquake better than a stiff and heavy one.

The paper used in building a Japanese house is not thin like the pages of this book. It is strong and thick and waterproof. The frame of the house is of wood, and the roof is often thatched with straw or covered with tiles. The roof may turn up at the corners as some Chinese roofs do. The corners that turn up are supposed to confuse bad spirits. If a bad spirit lands on the roof, it must follow the upward curve of the corners and fly off again.

The inside walls of the Japanese house are really moving panels. The family can slide them back and forth and make one large room or several small ones. The floors are covered with straw mats instead of rugs. When you enter the home of a Japanese you take off your shoes because no one wears shoes in the house. You can tell how many people are visiting or at home by counting the pairs of shoes outside.

The Japanese family eat sitting before little tables on the floor. They use chopsticks instead of knives and forks. When the mother cooks the food she chops it small enough to pick up with the chopsticks.

At night everybody sleeps on the floor. Instead

of beds, soft pads are used. Instead of a pillow, the Japanese put a carved little wooden block under their heads.

The family bathes in a wooden tub. Sometimes the tub has a charcoal burner under it to keep the water hot. Japanese bathers like their bath water much hotter than we do. If the family does not keep a bathtub at home, they may bathe at a public bathhouse.

Behind the wood-and-paper home is the family garden. The Japanese love small and beautiful things. Every garden has a pool, a tiny arched bridge, a stone lantern or two, and lovely flowers growing between ancient little trees that may be hundreds of years old.

There are houses in trees, houses on the ground, houses on cliffs, houses on stilts, and houses on the water. Now we find out something about houses on wheels.

A long time ago, a mysterious people came from India and spread out all over the world. These people we now call gypsies. They are a gay, music-loving people. They would rather travel along the road than stay in one place all of their lives.

Gypsies still live in caravans — brightly painted wagons that serve them as homes. They eat and sleep

Modern Cars have replaced the Gypsy Wagon

in these wagons while on their travels. We have many gypsies here in America, but they have changed with the times and now ride in automobiles. But the women and girls and some of the men still dress in gay costumes. To make a living, the gypsies help a farmer with his harvest or do odd jobs for people along the way. But when the job is done they want to roll again.

Gypsies are not the only people who travel and live in rolling homes. There are hundreds of thousands of people in the United States who live in trailers. You have seen these silvery houses on wheels pulled along our roads by automobiles.

Some people like to travel in trailers because they save money on hotel bills. Others, like the gypsies,

American Trailer

are restless and want to be able to move to new places. Still others, when they retire from business, live in trailers and follow warm weather. In winter they go South or Southwest or to the Far West. In spring you find their trailers in the cool Northern mountains or near beaches.

Some people also live in trailers because of their work. When a big factory opens and thousands of workers come for jobs, sometimes there are not enough houses for them to live in. So they buy a trailer and live in it instead of buying a house.

After the war, many thousands of students who

had been in service took advantage of the free education given them by the government. There were so
many of them that there were not enough houses to
go around. So the students, like the workers, bought
trailers to live in until they finished their college education.

The trailer is the first home made of metal that we
have met thus far. Most trailers are made of aluminum because it is strong and light. Inside, beds that
fold up against the wall, cooking stoves that burn
bottled gas, bathrooms with a shower, and refrigera-
tors to keep food cold make a well-equipped trailer
as comfortable as a house, although a bit cramped at
times.

Another metal home is the Quonset hut. These

Quonset Hut

half-round houses of ribbed steel came into being in World War II. We needed many thousands of buildings for military use — houses that could be made and put up quickly. The Quonset hut was the answer. After the war, many people bought these metal houses to live in, and in many parts of the United States you can see whole towns of Quonset huts.

Looking back at the unusual homes of the world, we can see that they resulted from a special need of the people who built them. Sometimes that need was fear of earthquakes. Sometimes it may have been high land taxes. Sometimes it was because a man's work forced him to go with it, as in barge-living or lighthouse-keeping. But each one made his home the best way he could.

River Flatboat

Cave dwellers

Now that we have visited some unusual homes, we want to find out how people got the idea of living in shelters, and then simple houses. Why did they feel it necessary to make a house? What materials did they use and where did they find them? What did they have to do to change the materials so that they could use them?

In this story of people and the homes they have made and lived in, we will try to answer some very important questions:

1. Why do people need homes to live in? When we study how the Egyptians lived, ask yourself, "Why didn't they live in log cabins or tents, instead of brick houses?"

2. How do people make their homes? What conditions help them make up their minds what materials to use?

3. How would it feel to live in homes of many lands and other times? Would it be cool or hot, dusty or smoky, dark or light, crowded or spacious?

4. What kind of family life did the people have

in the homes they built? What did they do
about cooking, eating, sleeping, bathing?
What did they do for a living and how did it
affect the kind of house they lived in?

5. Did the weather make any difference to people who planned houses? Would you build
a mud house in a land where it rains a great
deal? Would you live in a grass house if you
knew it would be very snowy and cold in the
winter?

6. How does the kind of country help people in
choosing the home they make? Would you
plan a log cabin on treeless plains or a stone
house in the middle of a sandy desert?

7. How did the invention of tools make home
building easier and better? How do modern
inventions improve the way we live in our
modern homes? What inventions can you
think of that might have made life less hard
for the people who lived in caves, castles,
Indian pueblos, or tents?

When we know the answers to all of these questions, we will know a great deal about people and
houses. We can learn still more by making little
models of these houses. Throughout this story you
will find easy directions on how to make models of

such simple houses as the sun-baked brick house of the early Egyptians, the adobe house of the Pueblo Indians, the tipi of the Plains Indians, the snow igloo of the Eskimo, and even a log cabin of the kind our American pioneers lived in.

Pioneer Cabin

The Eskimo boy, living in a house made of snow, would have no need for running water from a kitchen sink. He would cheerfully expect to melt ice or snow for any water he wanted. A little girl on a South Sea island, who lives in a grass house, would not miss the radio or television. She would not have heard about either. She would not need a bathtub, with the whole Pacific Ocean at her door to bathe and swim in.

With all the above seven questions in mind, let us try to go as far back as we can, to the time, many thousands of years ago, when people did not know how to build a house.

A very long time ago there were no houses on the earth at all. The people who lived at that time had no guns or knives. They killed animals with stones or crude spears and used the flesh for food. They ate what fish they could catch. They ate fruits and berries when they could find them.

There were no knives or forks or dishes. The men and women and children tore their uncooked food apart with their fingers and teeth.

We would think these people rough and unfriendly. They were afraid of the things they did not know or understand and they knew and understood very little. We do not think that they lived at first in families such as ours. They followed a strong leader who was able to defend them against the many enemies they had. Each group, with its leader, must have lived in fear, and apart from others of their kind.

The groups spent their days in hunting for food. No one had learned how to raise food or to store it for winter. Often food was very hard to find and the people had to go long distances before they could find anything to eat.

At first they climbed into trees to sleep. Then they huddled in groups on the ground. At last the increasingly cold winters forced them to discover that a cave was good to creep into for protection from the wind, the rain, and the snow. These caves were very uncomfortable and damp. Sometimes the men rolled large stones into the doors of their caves to keep out prowling animals who were also looking for food and shelter. Many of these caves in which early man lived have been found in western Europe, particularly France and Spain.

Modern Chinese Cave Dwellers

Many of the strange animals that lived at this time no longer exist. There were rhinoceroses with horns three feet long. There were great brown cave bears and the fierce saber-toothed cats, a little like our tigers. There were great mammoths, animals related to our elephant, but with long hairy coats. Some of their tusks measured twenty feet in length.

As time passed, great mountains of ice, or glaciers as we know them, moved down from the North. Each year the winter was more bitter. The snowfall was heavier and the sun-loving animals wandered south where it was warmer. But some of the animals remained to keep man company. The mammoth grew a warm woolly undercoat. So did the woolly rhinoceros. The reindeer and the musk ox blew out their steaming breath on the frosty air.

Man's cave home was chilly and damp but it was better than a tree or the hard ground. We do not know how or when people found out how to use fire. Perhaps some man carried home a burning branch from some forest fire or touched a stick to the lava from an active volcano. But fire made the caves warmer and lighter to live in.

Hunting was better near the water because the animals came down to drink. It was easier for hunters to follow their prey along the river banks than it was to push through brush and forest. But when the people moved to caves they still came down to the water to hunt. Cliff caves were safer to live in because they were high above the trails of fierce animals.

Hunters found that a sharp blade killed more readily than a clumsy wooden spear or stone hand ax. They found that a polished handle was easier to work with than a rough one. They began to sharpen and polish their crude tools and weapons.

People learned how to skin animals and to scrape and dry the hides. Skins were hung at cave entrances for protection from the sharp winds and rains. They also were made into clothing for the members of the family group.

Before the discovery of fire, people ate their food raw. But once they had tasted meat that had been scorched by flame, they found the full flavor of the cooked flesh delicious. From then on, they roasted meat over their open fires before they ate it. They

found that other foods — fruits, roots, and nuts — tasted better when touched by fire.

Women had hunted with the men. Now that they had fire, they were afraid to leave it untended in the caves. Fire was hard to carry about and no one had yet found a way to remake a fire when it had gone out.

The women and children stayed home to take care of the fire. The cave became a fixed place to live in. For the first time, people had real homes. The cave became a place where food was cooked. The men kept their tools and weapons in the cave. Tired hunters came back from the chase to enjoy hot food, warmth, and comfort.

Wild animals were afraid of the fires in the caves,

and now family groups lived in greater safety than ever before.

Tending the fire did not take all of the time of the women and children. They spread dried grasses and reeds on the floor of the cave to sleep on. They gathered wood and dried it out for future fires. They learned to plant and store a little food for winter. They found a way to shape crude baskets and pots to hold food and water.

In the long winter evenings, by the flickering fire-light, the men told and retold exciting stories of the hunt by making drawings on the hard stone walls of the cave. The women and children watched them carve out these pictures with sharp sticks and points of stone. They sometimes painted them with a mix-ture of animal fat and colors they scraped from the ashes of their fires or dug from the earth. Some of these wall decorations are very beautiful and show that some of these early artists had great talent. We can see pictures of these wall paintings in some of our museums.

Cave Painting

Homes in trees

At the same time that the people of Europe were finding shelter against the cold weather in caves, people in warmer parts of the world like Africa and Asia were living in houses they made in the trees.

A cave dweller had to live where his cave happened to be. A tree dweller could choose where he wanted to make his tree house. He could build near water and good hunting. His home had plenty of air and light. He was safe from most prowling animals. He was fairly cool in hot weather and his home gave him a good lookout over the countryside.

Enemies could track men to a cave hideout and trap them so that they were not able to escape. But a tree dwelling is not as noticeable as a cave. There is a better chance of fighting off an enemy from a high place. There is also more chance to get away.

These early tree homes were simple affairs. They must have been from ten to fifteen feet from the ground, judging from primitive tree houses still in use today. At night, ladders or climbing poles could be pulled up for protection from animals or in case of attack.

The floors of the tree house were made of bamboo or of branches lashed together and tied to the tree limbs with rattan or some other strong plant material. The roofs and walls were woven of long leaves or grass that kept out the glare of the sun in summer and the rain and wind of winter.

Philippine Tree Home

Modern tree dwellers live in many parts of the world today. Many natives of the Philippine Islands and New Guinea still live in trees. They make their homes in about the same way that their ancestors did. They cook in clay pots that hang from poles that hold up the roof. Thus there is less danger of setting the house on fire than there would be in cooking on a floor fireplace.

Living in trees seems such a natural thing to do that many children, from Maine to California, like to build simple tree houses of their own. A tree house makes a cool leafy perch to play in. It is easy to see, once you have been in such a house yourself, why so many people in the history of house building have found safety and comfort in tree homes.

Lake dwellers

When families ceased to roam, they learned to know each other much better. They became more friendly and no longer lived apart in fear of each other. They slowly formed villages to plant crops, to spin and weave, to develop the new art of potterymaking, and to exchange the things they made and grew with each other.

About seven thousand years ago there was a very important invention. People found out how to make an ax. This may not sound like much of an invention. But the long-handled ax made it possible for people to cut timber, build log houses, and to get out of their dark caves and mix with each other. The first axes with handles could not have been much more than a sharp-edged piece of stone bound to a long stick. Later a hole was bored in the axhead for the stick to fit in. Much later, axheads were made of bronze.

Along the shores of Lake Geneva, in Switzerland, we have found traces of people who lived there about seven thousand years ago. They built whole villages along the shore. The houses were set up on poles or piles to keep the homes high above the water where they were safely out of reach of floods and animals.

These homes were made of wattle and daub — a name we give to matted or interwoven twigs plastered with mud. The frames of the Lake Dwellers' houses were of timbers and the roofs of thatch, or long bundles of grass, laid one over the other to keep out the rain.

Fishing was easy from these homes over water. The people cleaned their fish and tossed the refuse into the water. Boats carried the house owners about the village and to and from other parts of the lake.

There was little furniture in a lake house. Crocks that held milk and cheese hung from the rafters so that most of the ants and other insects could not get in. Beds were made of rushes. Rope was not known by the people but they made nets from the fiber of

the flax plant. They used the nets to catch birds. Flax fiber was also made into a rough cloth for clothing. The people still wore garments made of the skins of the animals they hunted. We use flax today in the making of fine linen for clothing, for tablecloths, and for napkins. We also wear animal skins in the form of fur coats, belts, shoes, and leather gloves.

Not all of the villages were built near lakes. Small communities sprang up all over the earth. The homes in these communities were seldom more than simple huts, for tools were scarce. Men had to make use of whatever building materials they had at hand, and their houses were made to suit the climate where they lived. That is one reason why there are so many different styles of homes throughout the world.

In some parts of the world where it is always

Swiss Lake Village

warm, homes were made of grass or of leaves. In others, they were made of bamboo. Where there was no bamboo or grass and the climate was colder, houses were made of logs or of stone or earth.

Ruins of Andes Stone Hut in Peru

In some places there were no stones and no trees grew. Here the people made homes of dried mud or of clay. In desert lands, the shepherds made their homes from the hides of animals.

People in these different communities learned that they could capture wild animals and keep them alive. This gave them a sure food supply. They kept their animals in the houses where they themselves lived. Sometimes they made enclosures for them near their houses. Even today, far out in the country parts of France or of Holland or Belgium, the barns are joined to the houses. The stock does not actually live in the same room with the family, but the farmer will tell you that the heat from their bodies helps heat the whole house!

Horses, oxen, sheep, goats, and pigs were among the first animals to become part of the family household. These animals were fed and cared for and usually killed only when food was needed, just as they are on any farm today. The wild dog was also tamed to help people with the hunting and to help protect their homes and belongings.

People began to sow small fields with wheat, barley, and millet. The women roasted the grain when it had been gathered and ground it between stones. Then it was stored in earthenware jars or pots and saved until it was needed. The first bread was made when a woman found out how to mix this coarse flour with water or milk and cook it into a loaf.

The men showed the boys how to make axes, spears, and bows and arrows. They learned how to play too. First they played at hunting. Then they learned how to fish and to kill animals for food. The girls also helped their mothers with the care of the home. They learned from their mothers how to spin, to weave, to dress skins, to make clothing, to cook, and to take care of their younger brothers and sisters.

They did not spend all of their time at work. Men, women, and children loved to dance to the rhythm of earthenware drums made by stretching a skin over the top of a pot. They also learned to make and play rattles and whistles. They liked the sound of the music they made.

Men and women wanted the things they owned to be beautiful as well as useful. They decorated their pottery and carved the handles of the tools and the weapons they used. They designed bracelets and necklaces for their own adornment. They even invented what we call the safety pin to hold their garments together.

We still find ruins of ancient dwellings in all parts of the world. In them are the remains of many different types of weapons, tools, pottery, ornaments, and other objects used by the owners. By finding such ruins and studying what we can dig up in them, we have learned much about the people who lived such a long time ago.

People who live in grass houses

Far back in time, some people who lived in a warm climate found out that grass houses were easy to make and comfortable to live in. Some built their grass houses on the solid earth. Others remembered the safety of the trees and put theirs on stilts.

A stilt house is even better than a tree house. It can be made exactly where it is wanted. Stilt-house builders did not have to depend on the way the trees grew. All they needed were trees near enough to cut to make stilts. A stilt house could be made bigger than a tree house, with plenty of room for a family to move around. A stilt house would not sway in the wind as the tree house did.

Stilt houses are mounted on posts that are driven

Ainu Grass Hut on Stilts

firmly into the ground. The walls are usually woven of grasses and the roof thatched with leaves. As is true of the tree house, ladders or climbing poles permit the dwellers to go up and down and at night can be pulled up for safety.

People still live in stilt houses in many parts of the world. In Borneo, the Philippine Islands, New Guinea, and India the natives keep their animals and supplies under their houses and live over them. Simple fences of sticks keep household animals in and wild animals out.

Cooking, as in the tree house, is often done in a clay cooking pot. Some houses have fireplaces lined with clay or metal to keep the grassy surroundings from catching fire.

Some stilt-house people even enjoy running water in their homes. They put up pipes of bamboo that catch the water from cold streams that come from the hills in back of the village. We know that water will not run uphill, so it runs downhill and into the home.

Some New Guinea natives, like the early Lake Dwellers, put their houses on piles or long poles driven into the ground. The natives live on the edge of tidal salt water. When the tide comes in, the land under the houses is flooded. When the tide goes out, it takes with it all the refuse the people throw into the water. These New Guinea natives like to visit with each other, so they build plank walks to the houses of their neighbors. They also have catwalks or little narrow bridges to the dry land.

Even in our own United States we have a kind of stilt house. In parts of the country where the weather gets very hot in the summer, the people do not have cellars. Instead, they make their wooden houses on tall brick pillars so that fresh air passes under the house and helps to cool it off. There are many such houses in our Southern states and many northern summer houses are so built.

Food Storage on Stilts

Grass houses built on the ground are usually found in countries where there is much grass and few trees tall enough or strong enough to make good stilts. You might think that a grass house would be weak and easily knocked over. But the Swazis, a tribe in southeast Africa, make whole villages of dome-shaped grass huts. These huts are so strongly woven that when it is time for spring cleaning, the natives just lift the huts and move them to a new location.

The frames for these huts are made of young, whippy trees and reeds. Then the frames are covered with fine long grass. A village is called a "kraal." We have taken the word, kraal, and made it "corral,"

meaning an enclosed place where horses are kept.

A model of a Swazi hut takes careful work and great patience. Thin branches are used to make the frame. You must find some tall, dry, yellow grass in an empty lot or a field. To imitate the reed sides of the Swazi hut, use the bottoms of the long grass stems. These may be twined in between the twig framework. To thatch the roof, gather thin grass between your thumb and forefinger and tie it in a little bundle. With a pair of scissors, trim all the bundles to the same length. Then lay a row of grass bundles all around the roof frame, tying them in place with thread. The next row of bundles overlaps the first, and so on, to the point of the roof. Even a little thatch like this will shed water. Pour some from a water sprinkler. If you have done a good job, you will find that no water leaks into your thatched hut. (See diagrams below.)

When Christopher Columbus came to America on one of his voyages, he found an island tribe of Indians, the Caribs, living in grass-thatched huts on Dominica. The Spanish explorers had doubtless seen grass houses before in Africa but they must have been surprised to find them in the New World. But the Caribs, like the grass-building Swazis, lived in a warm climate and took the easiest building material around, which was an abundant supply of grass.

Model of Swazi Hut

Sod houses

Grass does not make a good building material for a cold climate. But if you cut out a piece of grass, roots and all, you have a sod — and sod makes a good building material for a warm house. We find many sod houses, both in the Old World and the New.

Chipaya Sod Huts of the Andes

In many parts of Ireland, farmers cut bog turf or sods to burn as fuel. Wood for both building and fuel is scarce. The majority of Irish homes, both in the city and in the country, are built solidly of stone. But if a farmer cannot get wood and there is not

55

enough stone around of the right size, the next best thing is to make a sod house.

He cuts out the grass-earth-and-root bricks with a sharp-edged shovel. Then he piles up house walls of the sod blocks, leaving openings for door and windows. His roof may be made of straw. To keep the straw roof on in windy weather, he ties it down with ropes made of twisted hay.

An Irish sod house is smoky inside because there is no chimney for the smoke to go out. It must go through the straw roof or out the windows or door.

Our own forefathers used sods to make temporary winter homes to keep them safe while winter

roared across the plains. As their wagons rolled west-
ward they saw that the trees grew fewer and fewer.
At last there were no trees at all. This meant that
they could not build log houses and their canvas-
covered wagons were not warm enough to live in
during the cold weather.

They used the only material they could find —
sods cut from the rich grassy plains. First they dug
down deep and then piled up the sod walls. With
the few boards they had, they made a roof support or
platform and piled it with more sods. If they owned
a section of stovepipe they stuck it through the roof
to let the smoke of their cooking and heating fire
escape.

Some of these plains sod houses were dug down
so deep that the family had to climb in and out of
them. But when the howling winter winds drove the
snow into huge drifts over them, they were safe and
warm. When spring came, they moved west again.

Alaskan Trapper's Sod House

The Navajo Indian, who lives in the southwestern part of the United States, sometimes uses sods to make his home. He calls it a hogan. In the summer he does not live in a hogan because he herds his sheep and must move from place to place to find enough grass for them to eat. While he is on the go he puts up an easy-to-build grass or brush shelter. But when winter comes he makes a six-sided hogan.

Navajo Hogan

First he drives heavy posts into the ground, then places lighter timbers across them for his framework. Then he piles the sods for his walls. To let out the smoke he cuts a hole in the brush-and-earth roof.

There are no windows in the hogan. The door opening is usually covered with a blanket.

Many people in the southwestern part of the United States are building sod houses as they were made hundreds of years ago when the Spaniards explored this part of our country. They found that sod from river bottoms is rich in clay. When such clay-rich sods are cut, they are full of tiny rootlets as fine as hair. When dry, these sod blocks are very strong. There are old Spanish church buildings made of such sods that are hundreds of years old and are still in use.

These modern sod houses are called "terron." They are built on poured concrete bases and look very much like Pueblo Indian adobe houses that we will learn about later.

Adobe and mud houses

After people had learned to make simple houses of branches and twigs, they began to experiment. One of these building experiments was to smear mud on the walls of interwoven branches and twigs. You remember that the Lake Dwellers used that type of construction and that we called it wattle and daub.

Everybody knows what mud is — a sticky mixture of earth or clay and water. But when you smear thickly mixed mud on loosely woven house walls and plaster it on thick, it changes the look and the "feel" of the house. When the thick mud plaster dries, it sticks strongly to the walls. The house is warmer in cold weather and cooler in warm weather. It is also harder for insects or for other animals to get in.

Mud is easy for people to find or to make. If there is water and earth at hand, mud can be made. But it is not a good building material if people live in a land that has much damp or rainy weather. That is one of the reasons why we find more mud-built houses in dry lands where there is much hot sunshine and little rain. A mud home in New Jersey or Ohio would soon melt in the rain.

Maya House of Mud

We do not know how long people have been using mud for their houses. We do know that the Lake Dwellers lived about seven thousand years ago and used mud in their wattle-and-daub huts. We know that people in Africa use mud to make their houses too. But we do not know when they began to make mud houses. More than likely they were using mud long before the Egyptians began to make bricks of clay and straw, mixed with water.

Natives in parts of the Belgian Congo in Africa

build fine mud houses. They stick young trees into the ground to make their framework. Smaller green sticks are woven between these props. This forms a mat or support for the mud that will be plastered on the walls. A grass roof is put on and the women mix clay with water and pat it into little cakes like mud pies. They press these mud cakes against the stick wall and smear them out to cover it. Then they wet their hands and smooth it all out. When the hot sun bakes the mud dry the house is ready to live in. Such a house will last for ten years or more.

Mud huts can be of many shapes. Some are made like half-round beehives. Others are carved, after the thick walls dry, into beautiful designs, like sculpture. In northern Africa, whole towns are made of dried mud.

Most mud houses have no windows. They are very simple inside. The floors are of hard-pounded earth. The people sleep on mats they make of grasses. Most of the cooking is done outside of the house because of the smoke.

From mud plaster to mud brick is a short step. Somewhere in the story of man's experiments with building materials, he found out that mud mixed with a little chopped grass or straw, then shaped into a brick, could be used for making fine houses. Some experts on house making think that the ancient Egyptians were the ones to find this out. We do know that the early Egyptians mixed mud with straw, put the mixture in molds, and let the sun dry it into hard bricks. They did not know yet how to put such bricks in a fire and burn them even harder. They let the sun do the work.

Wood was hard to find in Egypt. It was so scarce that the Egyptians used it only for house beams. The rest of the house was made of sun-dried brick. We use the term "adobe brick," meaning any brick made by mixing clay and water and straw, molding it into brick shape, and letting the sun dry it. The word "adobe" comes from a Spanish word meaning "to smear" or "to daub."

Like the hut of the African villager, the Egyptian house had no windows at all or a few very narrow

Early Egyptian Home

windows. The Egyptian did not want the sun to come through wide windows and heat up the inside of his house. He built the house with a flight of stairs going up on the outside to the roof. The roof was flat because there was little rain to be carried off. On warm nights, the Egyptian family went up to the roof to sleep.

Inside, the family cooked on an open hearth or fireplace. There were no stoves or chimneys to take the smoke away. It had to go out the windows, if there were any, and the door. Even in the richest Egyptian's home there were no chimneys. Servants scattered sweet-smelling oils and perfumes around to hide the odor of smoke and cooking.

It may seem a long jump from the sun-dried adobe brick of Egypt to the adobe brick house of the Pueblo Indians of our own Southwest. Before the Spanish came to America we think that the Indians

Hopi Adobe Home

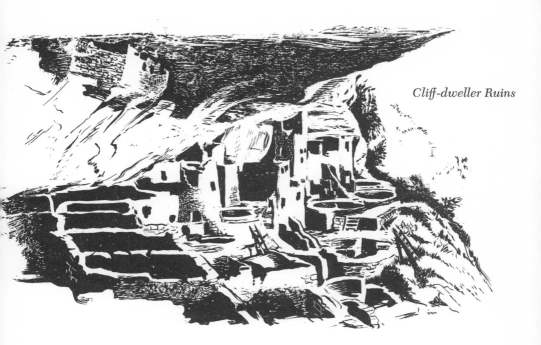

Cliff-dweller Ruins

of the Southwest used clay and stone for building but did not know how to make bricks. The Spanish, whose country was in close contact with northern Africa, used adobe brick to make their own homes in Spain. They may have shown the Indians how to mix clay and straw and water, how to mold the bricks, and how to put them in the sun to dry.

Like Egypt, much of Pueblo Indian country is hot and dry. Stone and clay are easy to find. Wood can be gotten from neighboring mountain slopes.

Long before the white man came to America, the Indians of the Southwest built great apartment houses of stone and clay. Some of them were perched high up under overhanging cliffs. Others were five stories high and as long as several of our modern city blocks. The Indians got from one story to the next by climbing a ladder. At night the ladders could be pulled up for safety and privacy.

Pueblo houses have few windows, perhaps for the same reason that early Egyptian houses had few windows. Too much sun coming into a house makes it very warm in the summertime. The Indians did their work on the stepped-back terraces of the houses and used the rooms only for sleeping. Here, on these terraces, women pounded corn into flour or ground it on a flat stone. They dried meat and vegetables in the hot sun. Today we still see Pueblo Indians doing about the same things and also weaving blankets and making pottery and fine jewelry.

In the Southwest today, many people are making their homes of adobe brick in the Indian style. They dig the clay out of their back yards and mold their own bricks. When the bricks are sun-baked, they make the walls. Peeled cedar logs are laid across the walls to hold up the roof. The roof is flat on top like the roof of the Egyptian house. When the house is finished it is very pleasant to live in. The thick walls keep the heat out in the summer and keep it inside in the winter.

Here is an interesting experiment. Find some clay near a brook or river bank. Cut up some grass into small pieces, using a pair of scissors. Mix a bowlful of clay, add a handful of the grass and enough water to make it thick enough to pat or mold into little bricks. When your bricks are made, put them in the sun to dry. (See diagrams below.)

When they are dry, make a model Indian home. You can use smooth sticks about as thick and long as a new pencil for your rafters. Lay the rafters across the walls, carefully place very fine twigs across the rafters, and then cover with a thick coating of mud to make the roof. If you stop here, you have made

Model of Adobe House

a model of a Pueblo Indian home. If you have enough bricks to build a little flight of steps up to the roof, you have an early Egyptian house.

If you are really ambitious, get some friends to help you make a five-story Pueblo home, complete with ladders so that your tenants can go from floor to floor. Follow the pictures in this book to find out how your model houses should look.

Also in the Southwest and in other warm sections of our country we can find Spanish houses whose style came here with the early Spanish explorers. These houses are not low like Indian houses but are two or three stories high. They are often combinations of stone to make the walls, plastered with adobe that is gayly colored.

The important part of the Spanish house is its patio, or inner court. The patio is a garden in the center of the house and surrounded by it. When it is hot, the family sits in the patio and enjoys the cool shade of trees and listens perhaps to the tinkle of a fountain surrounded by flowers.

Spanish Homes

Houses of brick

We know how the Egyptians and the Pueblo Indians made sun-dried bricks out of clay and water mixed with straw. Another people, the ancient Assyrians, made an improvement on sun-dried bricks, an invention that we still use today.

The Assyrians were a farming and pasturing people in the upper valley of the Tigris River. Their homes were very much like those of the Egyptians with whom they came in contact. But they found that if they put a sun-dried brick into a hot fire and then "burned" it, it became much harder and stronger than it was before. After they knew how to make fired bricks, they found out how to burn a glasslike coating on their burned bricks. We call bricks like these "glazed bricks." With them they made colorful pictures of their kings and nobles, sometimes hunting lions in chariots.

The ordinary Assyrian did not live in a fired-brick house. He still baked his bricks in the sun. Like the Egyptian houses, the Assyrian house was flat on top because the family used the roof for a bedroom on hot nights.

The Assyrian even had a primitive way of air-conditioning himself in hot weather. The house owner had a thick wool tent put up. While he sat inside it, his servants poured jars of water over the wool, keeping it wet. The hot sun dried off the water, making it cooler in the tent.

The kings and nobles of Assyria lived in wonderful palaces. In these palaces the walls were sometimes glazed in patterns that made beautiful pictures. Some of our museums have been able to obtain wall pictures that are just as bright now as they were when they were made thousands of years ago.

The knowledge of brickmaking spread all over the world. Brick is a good material to use if stone is hard to get or costs too much. If wood is scarce, then brick may take its place too.

There are many brick buildings in western Europe. The forests that grow there now are not large enough to supply all the wood that is needed for houses. In Scandinavia — Norway and Sweden — there are great forests, and many of the houses are made of wood. But it costs a great deal to buy lumber from another country and to ship it. So brick is very common as a European building material.

In Holland, for example, where wood is hard to get, there are many pretty little brick houses. The very old ones — houses made three or four hundred years ago — sometimes have odd-shaped roofs. Some of them look like old-fashioned clocks in front and in back and are called "clock-roofs." Others are shaped like rising steps and are called "step-roofs."

We use much brick in home building in the United States. Whole houses are made of brick. Brick is also used as a "curtain," or cover, on skyscraper apartment houses.

A brick house is warm in winter and cool in summer. Many brick houses have double walls, with an air space between the walls. Such brick houses are very comfortable because the air space is an insulator and keeps winter heat in and summer heat out.

In olden times people found much of their clay for bricks near rivers. Today many of our own brickyards are also near rivers because the clay from which the bricks are made is found in river banks and beds. Also, the finished bricks are often taken from the yards to the building contractors on barges. You may see long strings of brick barges, piled high with the red or yellow bricks, pulled by strong little tugs. We have read about the people who make their homes on barges in the chapter on unusual homes.

Houses of stone

The cave dwellers lived in what we might call stone houses, but they did not make them themselves. They found them already carved out of limestone cliffs by

Otowi Cave Dwellings, New Mexico

the action of water or of wind. A long time after the cave dwellers, people began to use stone for their homes. Because stone is so heavy and so hard to shape, they did not use it unless they could find it nearby.

Portuguese Stone House

At first, builders took pieces and chunks of stone as they found them. They did not know how to cut stone into blocks. But when people found out how to make even the simplest tools — hammers and drills and scrapers of hard stone — they were able to peck and hammer away at a big rock until they had shaped it into smaller pieces.

One of the oldest people who were remarkable builders in stone were the ancient Inca Indians. When the Spanish came to South America over four hundred years ago they found the Incas of Peru still living in the Stone Age. Their only tools were those made of stone. One of their old villages, named Machu Picchu [match-oo-peach-oo], shows us how these Indians built.

The village formed a strong fort. Every house was made of dressed stone blocks. The Incas cut these blocks with nothing but their hand tools. They were so careful in making them that you cannot put the thin blade of a pocketknife between them today.

Machu Picchu was built on different levels. Each level was connected to the others by stone stairways. Each house had three-cornered stone end-walls over which heavy beams must have been laid for the roof. We think the roof was thatched with grass but we cannot be sure, because there are no traces to tell us what materials were used for roofing.

These old Incas were surprisingly modern. They built stone aqueducts or water-carrying devices to take water to pools outside their homes. They built terraces and planted gardens. They used a reddish plaster on their inside walls. All of these wonderful

Old Inca Stone Ruins

things were being done by the Incas when much of the rest of the world lived in very primitive shelters.

The more people experimented, the more they learned. Their tools became better, and they constantly invented new ones. Also, they wanted more and more things, not for use alone, but because they were lovely to look at. Even the most primitive man, after he had learned how to make a clay pot, sometimes dug his thumbnail into the wet clay to make a pleasing design.

So by the time we come upon the Greeks of some three thousand years ago, we find buildings in stone that showed the great advances people had made in going from brush lean-to shelters and caves to real homes with plenty of room for everyone.

At first the Greeks built their homes of wood. Their temples to their gods were of wood also; later the great tree trunks that held up the roof were replaced by the marvelous stone columns we recognize today.

The people of Athens lived in well-made houses of stone. The wall that faced the street was blank except for the door. People did not want to have to look out at the street, which was narrow, dirty, and dark. Instead of street windows, the Athenians had a court around which their houses were made. Off

Greek Stone House

the court, with its flowers and statues, were the other rooms of the house.

Winter in Greece is snowy and rainy. So the roof of the Greek house slanted to carry off snow and rain. The heating system in the home was not very fine. There were little more than cooking fires and pans of glowing coals to keep off the chill. But the house was cool and pleasant in summer.

There was a dining room, but instead of a large table, the members of the family had their own little tables on which their food was placed. Many people ate lying on one side on a comfortable couch.

There were separate bedrooms in the house, and one of the duties of a young Greek girl was to learn how to make beds. Most people went to bed when it got dark. But if they wanted to stay up they could light oil lamps or candles.

The Romans admired and copied many Greek ideas. Greek traders who visited Italy in their ships took with them much of the Greek way of doing things. They brought to the Romans beautiful lamps, vases, and furniture for decorating their homes. When the Romans captured Greeks in battle and made them slaves they learned from them the way Greeks lived in their homes — how they ate at table, what games the children played in the home, and what clothing they wore in Greece. In 146 B.C., when the Romans defeated the city of Corinth, they shipped loads of marble statuary and works of art home. Much of this found its way into Roman homes.

When Rome was the leading city of the known world, during the reign of Augustus Caesar (29 B.C. to 14 A.D.) it had all kinds of housing. The poor people lived in slums, or tenements. Some of these poor homes were seven stories high. Many of them were rebuilt from the stones taken from fine old houses whose owners had moved to a more attractive part of the city. There were few kitchens in these poor people's houses. Those who had no hearth to cook on could buy their dinners ready to eat at shops on the streets. We have shops and services like this today.

The better homes in Rome were as carefully planned as we would plan our homes. The Romans

A Roman Country Villa

had some very definite ideas about homemaking that seem very much up-to-date. They said that the bedroom must get light from the morning sun. Perhaps this helped the Roman schoolboy to wake up early. Bathrooms were sensibly put in the warmest part of the house. When the owner turned on the water in his bathroom, it came out hot! It was heated with a wood-burning boiler underneath.

Rome was, and is, cold in the winter. Many houses had a system of heating not too different from our very best methods. The Roman heating expert laid rows of earthenware pipes under the floor. Hot water or hot air was passed through these pipes and heated the floor. But with this very "modern" radiant floor heating, nobody had yet invented a stove for cooking.

The rich Roman's home was fine indeed. Made of stone, sometimes faced with fine slabs of marble, it boasted a tile roof, a sunroom, bedrooms for all the family and servants, a game room, a lounge room, a dining room that could be opened to the sunshine and air, and great gardens where the owner and his family and friends could wander about and admire the flowers and the statues from Greece.

By this time painting had become a fine art and the Roman walls were covered with paintings. They

were not done on canvas, however. They were
painted directly on the plaster of the walls. As the
Romans ate, they admired these paintings. They
copied the Greek fashion of eating lying down. Instead of having little tables for every guest, everybody ate at one big round table, with their couches
pulled up around it.

The great government of the Romans fell before
the invasions of stronger people who did not know
much about fine building. By the year 600 A.D. the
period we call the Dark Ages had begun, and was

to last until the eleventh century. Many of the improvements people had learned to make were forgotten.

Many stone buildings called castles were built from the eleventh century to the fourteenth century in western Europe. We call this time the Middle Ages, and it was a time when Europe was slowly recovering from the Dark Ages, when over a period of five hundred years fierce barbarians from Scandinavia (the Vikings), Moslem pirates, and other warriors raided and burned wherever they went.

When castles were built, people were again not too friendly. Kings, dukes, lords, and earls fought for power and for wealth. They erected castles to protect themselves from one another.

A castle was a fort where people lived. Around

European Castle

it was a tall, thick wall of stone, with towers from which soldiers could rain arrows on attackers. Inside, there were many buildings, all of heavy stone. The only way inside was across a moat or deep ditch of water that went all around the castle walls. A drawbridge could be pulled up so that no one could enter.

Some people lived outside the castle walls. Farmers needed land on which to plant crops and to graze their animals. In times of peace, villages sprang up close to the castle. But in times of war, the castle had to be able to get along without any outside help.

In the castle were shops where armor and weapons were made. There were cooks and servers, shoemakers to keep people's footwear in repair, clerks and tailors, soldiers, stablemen, the noble's family and friends, and even a little band of musicians to play while people feasted.

Because it was so large and because it was made of heavy stone, the castle was a cold and drafty place in the winter. When the freezing snow and icy rains fell and the cold winds blew, even the great fireplaces piled high with roaring logs did little to make people warm. The stone floors of the castle were cold, even when piled deep with straw or rushes. The stories we read about life in a castle are exciting, but it must actually have been pretty uncomfortable to live in one.

In America we have many fine stone houses. Some of the earliest were built by the Dutch settlers who came to what is now New York in 1623. These Dutch stone houses look very much like the ones that you can still see in Holland. But there was so much wood to be had in the great American forests that it was easier to build of wood than it was to cut stone.

Houses of wood

We think that the Lake Dwellers may have lived in the first wooden houses in Europe. But part of their houses were made of wattle and daub — interwoven branches plastered with mud. Because wood does not ordinarily last as long as stone or brick, we do not know too much about how very early wooden houses were made.

When you cut down a tree, you can do many things with it. You can use the logs as they are to make a log cabin. You can split or saw the logs into planks and make your house of them. People must have built log houses before they found out how to cut trees into boards.

Many of us have been given the impression that our Pilgrim fathers, when they landed on Plymouth Rock, built log cabins to live in. But they did not know how to make log dwellings, never having seen them while they were living in England and, later, in Holland. The first Pilgrim home was a rough affair. It was made by digging a square hole in the earth, then driving pointed logs down, side by side. The roof was made of thatch — bundles of grass overlapping one another to shed the rain. Log cabins were not known in America until people from Norway and Sweden came to the New World.

The log cabin was very well known in Scandinavia. As you remember, there was much wood there and little in the rest of Europe. When people from Scandinavia came to America, they brought their knowledge of cabin building with them.

The Norwegian farmhouse has not changed much in hundreds of years of building. The farmer makes his log house in about the same way it was made a long time ago. First he cuts his trees and lets them dry for a time.

Then he peels off the bark of all the logs. A peeled log is less likely to harbor insects that might eat the wood later. He hollows each log underneath so that when he puts one on top of the other, they fit tightly together. When the walls are put up, he looks for any chinks or cracks that might let in cold air. If he finds any, he stuffs them with moss.

The roof of the cabin is covered with sods of turf. Sometimes birchbark is laid over the sods. Often flowers grow right on the roof of the house because the earth sometimes contains or catches flower seeds.

The Norwegian farmer puts up many buildings

14th Century Norwegian Cabin

on his farm land. All are made as his house is made
— of peeled and fitted logs. He makes a barn for the
cattle, a shed for his tools, a building where animals
are butchered, a smokehouse, a bathing house, and
even a special little shed in which the family beer
is brewed.

The farmer and his family go to town very seldom, so they must make many things they need.
They make their own butter and cheese, they cobble
their shoes, they make some clothing, they knit
their socks, sweaters, and gloves. They carve dishes
and spoons out of wood and they work on skis for
fast travel over the winter snow. After a hard day's

work on the farm and an evening's labor on handicrafts, the family goes to bed in cupboard beds set in the wall, something like those still found in some parts of Holland.

The kitchen of the Norwegian farmhouse has no stove, that is, if it is an old-fashioned kitchen. It has, instead, a fireplace called a "peis." It is built in a corner of the room and there is a good-sized space behind it so that the farmer's wife can dry clothing or store her firewood there.

The hearthstone of the fireplace is knee-high, instead of being level with the floor. This makes it easier to tend the fire and to handle heavy cooking pots. To carry off the smoke, there is a large hood over the hearth, held up by a single wood or stone column.

People like our Norwegian farmer came to America and soon found that American trees made fine log cabins. After they came, our first English settlers learned from them how to build log cabins. If you are ever lucky enough to make a visit to Plymouth Rock, at Plymouth, Massachusetts, you will see a reconstructed house of the kind the Pilgrims made to protect them during the first bitter winter. You'd hardly call it a log cabin.

American pioneers, after they knew log-cabin

building, took the idea to any place in America where trees grew. Some of them spent their entire lives in log cabins. Some of our most noted presidents of the United States lived in log cabins, among them Abraham Lincoln.

Even today, many American families prefer to live in a log cabin rather than to live in a house made in any other fashion. This may be due partly to the fact that they live in regions of the country where lumber is hard to get or because their ancestors lived in log cabins.

Like the Norwegian farmer, the American cabin builder piles his logs to make his walls. Sometimes he leaves the bark on. Sometimes he leaves it off. After the walls are up, the builder shingles his roof. If he builds the old way, he makes his own shingles by splitting them off a short, thick chunk of cedar, using a broad hatchet.

The floor of the log cabin used to be of hard-pounded earth. Later the pioneers split long thin logs in half and laid them, flat side up. Modern log cabins are floored with boards.

To keep the cold and wind out of the cabin, the builder fills any chinks with mud, grass, or chopped hay. The pioneers heated their cabins by means of fireplaces built at one end. They made their fireplaces and chimneys of native stone. They cooked on the fireplace, using frying pans with little legs to stand in the ashes. Home-made furniture was of logs and included chairs, tables, and beds. Instead of springs, the beds were fitted with rope supports for mattresses filled with cornhusks or hay.

The pioneer family lived a fairly comfortable life in their cabin. It was warm enough to shelter them from the severe winters of the North and West, and cool and dry enough for the hot weather and hard rains of the South. Most important of all, it gave them a good home until enough people were attracted to come to live near by. Then the little community got together and made a sawmill. With a mill, they could cut lumber — planks, beams, and boards — and build more houses.

You can make a model log cabin using short lengths of sticks. To make the sticks fit snugly, cut a notch near each end. When you pile the "logs" to make your walls, they will fit tightly together. A long stick for a ridgepole will hold up your roof. You can make shingles by splitting off thin sections of soft pine with a carving knife. To lay shingles, you begin at the edge of the roof and work across and up to the peak. Each shingle must overlap to keep water from leaking into your house. When cutting sticks to serve as logs, don't forget to allow for doors and windows! (See diagram below.)

While watching people build their homes all over the world, we begin to see that particular houses are built because of special needs or special circum-

Model of Log Cabin

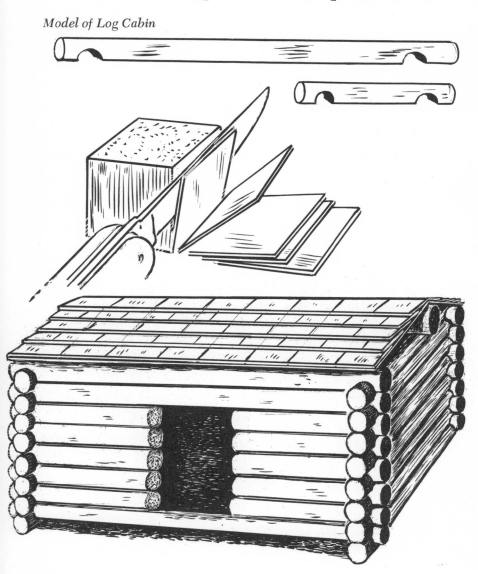

stances. The Norwegian farmer had plenty of logs on hand. The sod-building plains pioneer had no logs but had plenty of prairie from which to cut sods. The Egyptian had little wood for a house but he could find much clay to make sun-dried bricks. The African native living on the plains had grass all around him with which to make his house.

Now we come to a mountain people who must live out the winter in the Alps, as their ancestors did, where the snowfall is heavy, the winds are high, and snowslides, or avalanches, are not uncommon.

The Swiss mountaineer's chalet is the right house for the Alps. It is made almost square so that no matter how the wind blows, the pressure is about

Swiss Chalet

the same on any side it strikes. The timbers that make its walls are very heavy and thick. They are locked together outside the house walls. If a snow-slide roars down the mountain, the house has a better chance of holding up against it.

The chalet roof is very low and wide. It sticks out far past the walls so that blowing snow does not pile up against them. Shingles or heavy slabs of slate or stone cover the roof. Sometimes the winter storms are so wild that the family must lay heavy planks on the roof. They sometimes weigh down the planks with boulders to keep the roof from blowing off.

A chalet is a beautiful place in which to stay. In both summer and winter there is the mountain scenery to look at. When it storms, visitors feel safe because the builders made the chalet strong enough to stand firmly against it.

We have talked about houses made of logs and of timbers. Sometimes houses are also made of the bark of trees. The Eastern Woodland Indians lived in wigwams, or bark houses. As their name implies, they got their living from the forests along the Eastern Coast of the United States and from the many lakes and rivers and from the ocean. When the white man came to America, there were thick forests from which the Indians could take their building materials.

A wigwam is first framed with green young trees. One end is bent over and stuck deep into the ground. Then the other end is put in the ground to make an arch. The Indians tied wide strips of bark to the arched frame to make walls. The roof was also of bark and had a hole cut into it to let the fire smoke out.

Inside the wigwam, the Indians made platforms, running the length of both sides. These served as beds and were made comfortable with soft robes of rabbit or deer skin.

Chippewa Bark Houses

When the wigwam village was finished, the Indians sometimes put up a tall fence or stockade of sharpened poles. This stockade around the village kept it safe from attack by unfriendly Indians of other tribes.

The Iroquois made the largest bark houses. These Long Houses, as they were called, were sometimes one hundred and fifty feet long and twenty-five feet wide. Many families could live in one of them at the same time.

Another group of Indians who lived in great wooden houses were the Indians of the Northwest Coast. They lived on the Pacific Ocean side of North America, from northern California to Alaska. Great forests of cedar, fir, spruce, and hemlock gave them the materials from which to make their homes.

The Northwest Coast people knew how to split huge planks and timbers from trees without cutting them down first. They made tall platforms that stood against the trees. Then they split the planks off, using wedges and their primitive hand tools.

These huge houses were usually built in rows, facing the water. Some of them were as large as sixty feet by fifty feet. The frame was made of heavy beams and posts. The walls and roof were made of split cedar planks.

Inside the house, the Indians made two terraces, each about six feet wide. These terraces ran all around the house. They were divided into little "apartments" by hanging blankets or screens. The families lived in them and kept their belongings there. In the center of each house was a fireplace where cooking was done.

Long ago, the Northwest Coast people learned how to cook in wooden boxes. They bent planks with steam and hot water and then "sewed" the wood together with strong thread made of spruce roots. By putting food and water into this wooden "pot," and then dropping in heated stones, they could cook their food.

They ate from hand-carved wooden dishes and used spoons made of horn. They also made totem poles that stood outside their houses. These tall poles, with their odd-looking carved animals, were made to tell the history of the family, what clan they belonged to, or to serve as a remembrance of former members of the group.

Since the Indians have come more closely into contact with the white man and his belongings, fewer and fewer of them know the old skills. They now cook in metal pots, use tools made of steel, and buy much of what they need from stores. But they still can do wonderful carving in wood and in black slate and horn, and they make strong and lovely baskets of spruce-root fibers.

Homes in dangerous places

Before we go on to the familiar homes of our own United States, let's pause to look at some homes in dangerous places. Many people in this world live in homes that are permanent only as long as Nature lets them be. Sometimes people choose places in which to live that seem to be a constant threat to safety. But these people have their reasons for choosing such sites.

The edge of a slope of a volcano that blows up once in a while is not a safe spot for homemaking. But the soil around volcanoes is very rich. It grows wonderful crops. For many hundreds of years, Italian grape growers have lived on the very sides of active volcanoes. They hope that the fiery mountain will not erupt and destroy their homes. Sometimes these volcanoes do become active. Then the homes and the grape arbors are buried under tons of ash or lava. But when the volcano is quiet again, the people come back to rebuild and to till the rich soil.

The Bataks of Sumatra often make their homes on volcanic slopes because of the rich earth. These houses look like big Noah's Arks on stilts. They often have double roofs. Like the Italian farmers, the Bataks hope that the next volcanic eruption will

Batak Stilt Houses

not harm them. When it does come, they return to build.

Volcanoes are dangerous enough, but living near rivers that spill over in great floods is just as perilous. Many people, Americans as well as people of other countries, have built their homes near rivers that sometimes leave their banks. Then homes, stock, crops, and people are endangered.

Some of these people have to live near dangerous rivers because they do not have money enough to live in safer, higher parts of town. Other people own their own land near the river and do not want to leave it. After a flood many of the people go back to their homes if they are still left standing. They clean out the mud, make repairs, and hope that another flood will not come.

The Dutch people live in a part of the world where the land is sometimes twenty feet below the level of the sea. To keep the sea out they have made great dikes of earth, stone, cement, and steel. A system of windmills pumps surface water from one canal to the next, always raising it higher. At last the water is pumped into the sea.

But when great storms come, the giant waves punch holes in the dikes. Then the dry land is flooded with salt water. People lose their lives and their homes. It takes a long time to rebuild an area flooded by salt water. Crops will not grow until the salt has been washed out of the soil.

Another danger to homes is high wind. People who live where hurricanes or cyclones are common almost get used to them. When the weather bureau warns them a hurricane is on its way, they board up all the windows and tie everything down. Then they lay in a supply of food and candles and wait out the storm. When it has blown itself out they clean up and carry on their regular business of living.

People who live in parts of the country where tornadoes are common are also used to living with them. A tornado is a funnel-shaped whirling mass of air that sucks up and destroys as it roars along a narrow path. In tornado country the people dig deep cellars with heavy doors. When they know the tornado is coming, they duck into their cellars and wait for it to go by, hoping, in the meantime, that it misses their property.

Portuguese House Braced for Quakes

There are many other dangers that threaten people where they live. In countries like India, the danger of being bitten by poisonous snakes is very great. In other parts of India, in the country, wild animals like tigers and leopards make life hazardous. In lion country in Africa there is some danger of finding a lion in your living room. Elephants might wander into your garden and destroy not only your crop but your house as well.

People who live in dry grassy country are in danger of grass fires that roar like an express train when there has been no rain. People living in forests must think of forest fires. But no matter what the danger, people continue to live in what we consider dangerous locations, and they have good reasons for not wanting to leave their homes.

American homes of today

Because our nation is made up of people who have come from all over the world, all of our houses are not alike. In an African village, where all of the natives are of one tribe and follow the same customs, all of the houses will be alike. Even the chief's house will be of the same design, but perhaps larger.

Because the climate of the United States is not the same all over, our houses are also built to suit the kind of weather they will have to stand. Much of the country, during the winter months, is covered with deep snow. It rains a great deal in other parts of the land during the winter. We have mountains and deserts and seacoast and lake coast, and our houses vary in design with the differences in location.

When we were a very young nation, our forefathers had only recently come from the Old World. They loved the new land but they still remembered the old. So, to remind them of England or of Holland or of Germany or of Norway, they made their houses a little like those they had left behind in the old country.

103

English Timbered House

Men and women who came from England remembered the dwellings they used to live in. When
they could set up a sawmill to cut timber, they made
some of these old-style English houses with their
thatched roofs. They were lovely to see, with their
soft sloping lines and leaded windowpanes. But
the American winters were much colder than English
winters. The English-Americans had to cover their
pretty homes with overlapping boards, called clap-
boards, to keep out wind and cold.

There was little machinery in the new land. Even
the common nail had to be made by hand. Nails

were used only to fasten the long flat boards to the frame of the house. The sturdy beams that held up the roof and floors were pegged together. To peg a beam or timber, the workman bored a hole through the beam he wished to fasten to another beam. He continued to bore his hole halfway into the second beam. Then he drove a stout hardwood dowel or rod of maple or of oak into the hole. There are some pegged houses standing today that are hundreds of years old and they are still so strong that they will last many years more. You may see pegged beams in many old country barns. Look for the pegs at the beam ends the next time you are in an old farm building or barn.

The early American builders also had to make their shingles by hand. There were still no lumberyards where they could buy bundles of ready-cut roof coverings. To make shingles, they cut off wide, thin pieces of wood, usually of cedar. Such handmade shingles were called "shakes." Later, when the settlers found masses of bluish-gray rock we call slate, they split it into thin pieces and used them for making fine long-lasting roof coverings. Some of our finest houses are roofed with slate today.

Shingles must be put on the roof of the house so that the water from rain or from snow runs down and off the house, not into it. To make sure that happens, the roofer lays a row of shingles on the roof edge. The next row of shingles lap over the first, with the crack between shingles in the first row covered by a whole shingle. Each row of shingles all the way to the ridge of the roof is so placed. When it rains, the water runs down the shingles and into the rain gutters.

Dutch settlers in Nieuw Amsterdam, now New York, built their homes the way they had built them in Holland. They made many of them of stone and even sent back to Holland for the small Dutch red bricks that we still find in early Dutch homes today.

As our country grew, it had more time to build large and beautiful homes. Some were copied after Greek temples, with fine white columns standing in front. Still others were simple white frame houses that still stand like modest girls behind their white fences.

In the eighteen-hundreds, a style of house appeared that we call Victorian. This house was covered with "ginger-bread," not the kind you eat, but cut-out curly wooden trimmings and useless ornaments. The Victorian houses are not pretty but they are big enough for a large family and are still comfortable and spacious.

While the New England settlers were building English-style houses in the East, the Spanish settlers were out West, remembering the homes they had left in Madrid and Seville in Spain. The climate of the Southwest and California is warm like that of Spain. The Spanish people knew how to make houses that would be cool in summer. So they built Spanish-style houses with red or green tiled roofs and a cool patio where they could relax in comfort.

Some houses fit into their surroundings as though they had grown there. A Cape Cod fisherman's house nestles among the sand dunes and the beach grass. It becomes a part of the land- and seascape. A cattleman's one-story ranch house sprawls comfortably on the plains. But neither house looks quite right when it is built in the other's original location.

A farmer's house tells us that he needs plenty of room. He needs room for a large family and for hired hands to help him run his farm. The farmhouse kitchen must be large enough for his hardworking wife to cook huge meals on the big stove

American Farm

for hungry family and farm hands. The dining room and its table must be large enough to seat them all.

There are private little homes all over our land — in the cities, in the towns, and in the villages. They are perhaps the most important homes because most Americans live in them. They are of all styles of

building, they are sometimes expensive and sometimes very low in price. But no matter what they
look like or what they cost, they are important because the people in them own a bit of America.

Mount Vernon

Not all the people who live in cities can have
their own homes. There is not enough room. When
many people live in one place they begin to crowd

each other. Soon there is no room to move sideways, so they have to move up. That is why there are more apartment houses in the cities than there are in towns and villages.

The apartment house is not an American invention. We know that the desert people of northern Africa live in large houses with many rooms. So did the Greeks, the Romans, many Europeans, and our own Pueblo Indians.

An American apartment house is usually taller than those in other countries because we are more crowded and also because we have more elevators to carry people to their rooms. It would be hard indeed to have to climb twenty or thirty stories to your home every night.

Modern apartment houses would not be possible without the use of steel. Without steel beams and girders, the walls would be so thick that there would hardly be room inside for living. With steel, we can make apartment houses twenty, thirty, forty stories high. If we wanted to, we could make an apartment house as high as the Empire State Building in New York City.

An apartment house needs even more materials than does a private house. There is the structural steel that supports the building. After the skeleton of steel is up, the rest of the building is made of stone, brick, glass, concrete, or metals like aluminum. The inside of a modern apartment house, once the building is up, resembles a private home but is on a much larger scale. Instead of installing one kitchen door, you must order perhaps three hundred or even three thousand. But even the apartment dweller tries to make his quarters seem like a private home, even though he may be surrounded by thousands of other families.

Apartment dwellers have less work to do than do people who own their own homes. When it snows, the superintendent cleans the walk. He also takes care of the furnaces and makes repairs that a home owner would have to do himself or hire someone else to do.

Apartment-house living is convenient and comfortable. But sometimes there is not enough room for children to play and not enough sense of owner-

Apartment Houses

ship to satisfy the people who live in apartments.

Let's sum up the story of people and their homes. In doing so, we have found the answers to the seven questions we asked ourselves in the beginning of the story.

1. People live in homes because they need shelter from cold and warm weather, from rain and from snow, and from wild animals, if there are any around. They need homes to work in, to store their tools in, to cook and to eat in, and to learn the games of children and the work of men and women.

2. They make their homes in all the ways that seem best to them. Some homes are large, others small. Some are round, cone-shaped, square, oblong, with one story, two stories, thirty stories. Some have curved roofs, some flat, some peaked. Some are on stilts, some on the water, many in trees. We know how they make their homes and we know why when we find the other answers to the other questions.

3. We know how it feels to sit around a fire in a smoky Tibetan yurt. We have smelled the perfume that servants scattered in Egyptian houses. Our feet have grown cold in wonderful but chilly castles. We have heard the thunder of buffalo outside our Plains Indian tipi, and we have almost heard the hot sun beat down on the Hopi pueblos.

No 4. We have lived with the families who have made homes all over the world. We tended fires with the cave people, fished from our front porch with the Lake Dwellers, helped dry corn and meat with the Indians, played games with Chinese boat children, and cleaned house with the pioneer family that lived in a log cabin.

No 5. We know that you cannot build a mud house in a land of much rain. We know that logs make warmer houses than grass, but that sods make warm winter houses too. We found that Pacific Island homes have no use for bathtubs or stoves and that snow provides our Eskimo friends with building material.

6. We know that people were influenced by the country they lived in. The kind of country helped them make up their minds as to what building material they were going to use. They knew that you could not build a log cabin on a treeless plain. They had better sense than to try to put up a stone house in a sandy desert. They knew that if they lived in thick forests they could make their homes of logs or of twigs or of branches or of bark. They used what the country gave them, whether it was grass or sods or clay or bamboo.

7. We found out that when people invented the

simplest tools of stone they were able to make better homes. When bronze took the place of stone and iron, and steel took the place of bronze, people could control their building materials better. They could make beams, planks, and boards of logs. They could cut and plane and bore and chip and polish their materials. We know that modern stonecutting machinery would have permitted the castle-building people of Europe to finish their work many years before they did. We also realize that inventions like modern heating and plumbing would have made the old Roman tenement more comfortable to live in. Air conditioning would have made the homes of Egypt and Assyria and the southwestern parts of our own land more livable.

To these answers, let's add one more question:

What does your home mean to you?

Here's some help in answering that eighth question.

No matter what kind of home you live in — an apartment house, ranch house, a cottage, or a palace

— you make your home by the way you live in it. The way you think and act makes your home. The friends you invite to visit you make your home. Your books and games and music make your home. And the most important thing of all is the love all of us give to and receive from our family.

Then we can say, "There's no place like home," and truly know what it means.

Modern American Home

Index

About the Author and Artist

Dr. William A. Burns has been interested in museums ever since he was a boy. Every time he arrives in a new city he always goes first to find out what its museum holds. He received his master's degree and doctorate at Columbia University. During the war he served in Hawaii, the Pacific Islands, New Caledonia, and Australia. In 1950 he was sent by the State Department to organize programs of museum education in the Dutch schools. He began his work with the American Museum of Natural History as a teacher and is now Assistant to the Director of the Museum.

Paula Hutchison was born in Montana and studied at the University of Washington and Pratt Institute. She later went abroad and for two years studied art in Florence, Paris, and London. She is now a member of the Illustration Corps at the American Museum of Natural History and is also well known for her decorative panels for architective display.